FORGIVE!

AS THE LORD FORGAVE *YOU*

Patrick H. Morison

Presbyterian and Reformed Publishing Company
Phillipsburg, New Jersey

Library of Congress Cataloging-in-Publication Data

Morison, Patrick H., 1937-
    Forgive! as the Lord forgave you.

    1. Forgiveness—Religious aspects—
Christianity.   I. Title.
BV4647.F55M67 1987   241'.4   87-6961
ISBN 0-87552-293-9

Martha sat staring sullenly at her pastor. "But it's not fair to tell me I must forgive Jim. You haven't had to live with him. He yells at me all the time. I know I'm not perfect, but I can never please him. Now he has spent all our savings to buy that expensive stereo. He said he wanted at least one nice thing in the house. Well, I work hard too. Why didn't he ask me first?

"When I told him he shouldn't have done it, he lost his temper again. You should have heard the things he said to me! And he claims he's a Christian. Real Christians don't do things like that.

"Now he says he's sorry and wants me to forgive him again. We've been through all this before, and I've had it. He can keep house for himself. He doesn't like the way I do it anyway. I can't forgive him."

Although we all would like our own sins forgiven, we often find it difficult to forgive others completely and genuinely, particularly when the offense has hurt us deeply or often. Yet Jesus teaches us to pray, "Forgive us our debts, as

3

we forgive our debtors" (Matt. 6:12, KJV). By calling sins "debts," Jesus pictures the sinner's moral obligation to pay the consequences for any offense against God or another person. Forgiveness grants release from that obligation. Instead of demanding a penalty, the forgiver—God or man—assumes the loss by setting aside his due. He extends mercy instead of judgment.

The call to forgive can actually add pain to the offense. Are we now to take on this additional burden for the sake of someone who hurt us in the first place? Is that reasonable? To the Christian brother or counselor who reminds us that God gives us no option but to forgive, we cry, "No! It's not fair!" Ultimately, however, our anger is against Christ, who makes this "unreasonable" demand. But if we will pursue the Lord's will, trusting that He knows more about these things than we do, we will discover that His way brings healing and peace.

How, then, can we submit our emotions and attitudes to the lordship of Christ? Although His command is simple, clear, and loving, our sinfulness, our unbelief, our conflicting feelings, and garbled communication make obeying difficult. We need both practical understanding and the inner discipline of the Holy Spirit. In what follows we will examine six aspects of the process to better our understanding. Let us also pray for the Spirit's filling so that we may begin living out His will. As we struggle to be faithful to forgive, we discover not our own accomplishments and generosity of spirit, but God's firm promises and grace.

I. BELIEVE THE PROMISE: FORGIVEN!

At the outset we must trust God's free grace in granting

us forgiveness. Our relationships with people reflect our true spiritual relationship with God. Knowing that Christ forgives and loves *you personally* is the experience of grace you need to genuinely and deeply forgive others. Jesus said, "He who has been forgiven little loves little" (Luke 7:47). Have *you* experienced deeply the grace of God? Or are you still groping to win His approval?

If you have little experience of or confidence in the life-changing power of God's grace, you will likely be ungracious in your demands of others. A critical spirit and negative expectations will dominate your relationships. Forgiveness and the desire to restore and build up others will be far from your mind. In general you will have little patience with the weaknesses of others, especially those close to you. When tensions arise, you will leap to your own defense while trying to pin the blame on others. You will tend to keep a safe distance from Christians whose lives reflect true love and holiness, lest they uncover your inner unworthiness. You might even go on the attack and find fault with them, in order to soothe your own conscience. This negative spirit generates further tensions and distrust, so as to invite others to strike back. In such an atmosphere trusting and joyful relationships, creativity, and loving ministry cannot flourish.

Perhaps you are reluctant to admit that you doubt God's grace if you have accepted the gospel publicly. Are you really certain Christ died for you? Has the truth gripped your heart that you have come to God, that He has pardoned you from the guilt of your sin, and that He has accepted you as His dear child? Or do you sense a tension between the gospel you have professed and the true feelings in your heart? Could these observations by J. C. Ryle fit you?

5

They never come to the point of actually laying hold on Christ by faith, and becoming one with Christ and Christ in them. They can say, He is a Savior, but not "my Savior,"—a Redeemer, but not "my Redeemer,"—a Priest, but not "my Priest,"—an Advocate, but not "my Advocate": and so they live and die unforgiven! No wonder that Martin Luther said, "Many are lost because they cannot use possessive pronouns" (Ryle, *Practical Religion*, p. 7).

How can we deal with this underlying uncertainty about God's grace to us? First, confess unbelief; then affirm God's promise of mercy:

> When the kindness and love of God our Savior appeared, he saved us, *not because of righteous things we had done, but because of his mercy* (Titus 3:4-5, emphasis added).

We cannot earn God's favor. Our sin has created an obligation we cannot possibly remove or satisfy by ourselves. The Spirit testifies,

> No one will be declared righteous in his sight by observing the law; rather through the law we become conscious of sin (Rom. 3:20).

A favorite gospel hymn puts it this way:

> Not the labors of my hands,
> Can fulfill Thy law's demands;
> Could my zeal no respite know,
> Could my tears for ever flow,
> All for sin could not atone;
> Thou must save, and Thou alone
> (Augustus Toplady, "Rock of Ages").

We must be absolutely clear on this point: we *can and need do nothing* to earn God's mercy; His forgiving love comes out of His freedom, at His initiative. He chose to give us value by saving us, investing the life and death of His Son to redeem us from the guilt and grief and death our sin brings us (see Eph. 1:3-10; I John 3:1-3; 4:9-10).

We need not earn the grace of God. And to attempt to do so by "doing righteous things" offends God's free grace. It denies His right to save whom and how He will. It distrusts His promise and discounts the saving work of Jesus Christ (see Rom. 9:30–10:13; Phil. 3:3-9). So then, we are not called to forgive others in order to earn God's love; rather, having experienced His love, we have the basis and motive to forgive others.

Having firmly grasped the free grace of God, we can confront our own sins not only by receiving pardon but also by turning away from them, by repenting. Unless one puts off habitual disobedience—including an unforgiving spirit—the comfort of forgiveness will be overshadowed by renewed guilt. God charges us to throw off these sinful patterns and replace them with new ones:

> Therefore each of you must put off falsehood and speak truthfully with his neighbor, for we are all members of one body. . . . He who has been stealing must steal no longer, but must work, doing something useful with his own hands, that he may have something to share with those in need. Do not let any unwholesome talk come out of your mouths, but only what is helpful for building others up according to their needs, that it may benefit those who listen. And do not grieve the Holy Spirit of God, with whom you were sealed for the day of redemption. Get rid of all bitterness, rage, and anger, brawling and slander, along with every form of malice (Eph. 4:25, 28-31).

As we persist in changing our lifestyles through faith, our appreciation of and confidence in God's mercy grows. We realize that Christ saves us not only to spare us divine judgment but also to set us free from sin's bondage (see Rom. 6). As you grow more confident that God's grace and power are working in *your* life, you also learn to trust His work in your brothers and sisters in Christ (see Phil. 1:6, 9-11; 2:12-13).

Moreover, as your confidence and faithfulness grow, you become more aware of needing God's loving correction and discipline. The Holy Spirit admonishes us:

> My son, do not despise the Lord's discipline and do not resent his rebuke, because the Lord disciplines those he loves, as a father the son he delights in (Prov. 3:11-12).

> Clothe yourselves with humility toward one another, because "God opposes the proud but gives grace to the humble." Humble yourselves, therefore, under God's mighty hand, that he may lift you up in due time. Cast all your anxiety on him because he cares for you. . . . And the God of all grace, who called you to his eternal glory in Christ, after you have suffered a little while, will himself restore you and make you strong, firm and steadfast (I Pet. 5:5b-7, 10).

This God-given self-humbling dissolves a hyper-critical or defensive, unforgiving spirit. Dissolving this spirit is crucial. God's loving, nurturing discipline often comes to us through fellow-disciples who teach, admonish, and even rebuke us with the Word of God. We must receive these as a ministry of divine grace, without taking offense, and learn from them.

Whoever loves discipline loves knowledge, but he who

hates correction is stupid. . . . The way of a fool seems right to him, but a wise man listens to advice (Prov. 12:1, 15).

As God administers His gracious discipline in your life and you begin to see the growth of the Spirit's fruit, you will learn to praise Him for the blessing of discipline (see Gal. 5:22-23; cf. John 15:1-5). You will begin to *experience* all things working together for good, confirming God's grace to you and strengthening your love for Him (see Rom. 5:1-5; 8:28-39). Forgiving others will become increasingly natural for you as your faith to receive God's forgiveness works itself out in freely forgiving others.

II. OBEY THE COMMAND: FORGIVE!

Trusting the Lord's grace, commit yourself to obey Jesus' command to forgive. Your obedience must not depend on how you feel toward the offender but on Jesus' example and command. Hear again His cry from the cross: "Father, forgive them, for they do not know what they are doing." Jesus' persecutors hated Him in their blind self-righteousness and were determined to destroy His work and life, to humiliate Him, to inflict as much pain as possible. Yet He prayed for their forgiveness, and He teaches us to pray, "Forgive us our sins, for we also forgive everyone who sins against us" (Luke 11:4).

Jesus makes the issue clear and crucial; it lies at the heart of our response to the gospel. We all need forgiveness:

If we claim to be without sin, we deceive ourselves. . . . If we confess our sins, he is faithful and just and will forgive us our sins and purify us from all unrighteousness (I John 1:8, 9).

9

However, in giving that promise, He insists that we forgive those who sin against us.

> If you forgive men when they sin against you, your heavenly Father will also forgive you. But if you do not forgive men their sins, your Father will not forgive your sins (Matt. 6:14-15).

Forgiveness is *not* simply ignoring something sinful, but for love's sake deliberately releasing the offender from his obligation to suffer the penalty and make restitution. A repentant offender may need to make restitution as a part of reconciliation, but our offer of forgiveness is not contingent on that.

Once we extend forgiveness, Jesus tells us to do even more: seek to restore trust and a healthy relationship. Without this, forgiveness remains theoretical. *Reconciliation* implements in our personal relationships the pattern of God's grace to us. God, having forgiven us, does not abandon us but unites us to Himself in continuing fellowship (see Rom. 5:1-11). Without reconciliation, we withdraw from the injured relationship and lose the opportunity to bless one another. Our first objective is to help our offender experience God's reconciling grace concretely through the healing of our relationship. The second objective, equally important, is to be reconciled for the sake of God's congregation, its unity, fellowship, ministry, and holiness (see Matt. 18:18-20).

Make no mistake, reconciliation often demands hard effort and long hours at working through the issues, both for the parties at odds and for those assisting them. Each must examine his own speech and behavior, his attitudes and motives. The *offended* person particularly must humbly consider what he may have contributed to the problem, and be willing to accept that responsibility rather than simply lay blame on the other. This is emotionally draining and humbling; it is a sacrifice. But, for all that, it is a work of grace and faithfulness, one way of laying down our lives for our friends as the Lord Jesus did (see John 15:12-14). If we refuse to work at this, ruptured fellowship, frustrated ministry, and division will continue to plague families and churches. No real forgiveness will take place; rather, people will grow depressed and even bitter. " 'Love your neighbor as yourself.' If you keep on biting and devouring each other, watch out or you will be destroyed by each other" (Gal. 5:14b-15). How can we "spur one another on to love and good deeds" (Heb. 10:24) if we allow hurts and sins to remain unresolved and brethren unreconciled?

But what if the erring brother refuses to be reconciled? Jesus tells us:

> If your brother sins against you, go and show him his fault, just between the two of you. If he listens to you, you have won your brother over. But if he will not listen, take one or two others along, so that "every matter may be established by the testimony of two or three witnesses." If he refuses to listen to them, tell it to the church; and if he refuses to listen to the church, treat him as you would a pagan or a tax collector (Matt. 18:15-17).

We are told to go back to the resistant brother with one or two others who can give counsel and an impartial account. If the brother still refuses to resolve the matter, then it must come before the congregation, either directly or through its elders, whom the Holy Spirit has ordained to judge disputes between believers (I Cor. 6:1-5). A church must not rush through these three steps mechanically in an eagerness to dismiss errant people. Rather, each step in church discipline requires careful attention to clear communication, persistent prayer, patience, and gentleness. If, however, all these efforts fail because a person refuses to be reconciled, the relationship must remain breached. Still you must maintain your willingness to forgive, while lovingly, and often with grief, you commit him to God for discipline or judgment. You have thus resolved the matter on your part (Matt. 18:17; Rom. 12:19; I Cor. 11:31-32). (Incidentally, this procedure also applies if you are the offender seeking forgiveness but are rebuffed [see Matt. 5:23-24]. Responsibility for initiative in resolving these problems lies with *both* sides, but especially with the one who first becomes aware that an offense has occurred.)

III.   TO RETALIATE OR FORGIVE?

''When they hurled their insults at [Jesus], he did not retaliate'' (I Pet. 2:23). Forgiving means refusing to retaliate. How do people retaliate? Physical or verbal abuse—hitting and shoving, yelling and cursing—are obvious examples. Christians sometimes do such things. However, because these are so blatantly sinful, Christians tend to substitute more restrained weapons, unless they lose self-control. But even restrained retaliation is sinful and harmful.

You can find all kinds of ways to retaliate, to get back at whoever has hurt you. One of the easiest is to *withdraw*. You simply deprive the other person of your company, plan your activities to avoid him, and hope he gets the message! (He probably will, although he often does not understand it, for which you can also blame him!) Withdrawal expresses your anger over the offense. It helps you hide the pain you feel, pain that cannot be genuinely healed as long as you disobey Jesus' will for reaching a resolution. By withdrawing you also quietly frustrate the life or work of your offender by being absent when he needs you. With this tactic you can hurt the other person without having to do anything, and without feeling responsible. Marriages, families, churches, and work places are common arenas for this kind of passive retaliation.

You can also retaliate by *complaining* against or criticizing people who have hurt you. This takes various forms. First, you may complain without offering any constructive thoughts or actions. Complaining becomes an end in itself, to vent bad feelings and ill will. Because this resolves nothing, it often deteriorates into whining or nagging. Frustration builds up emotional pressure, which may escalate into more serious retaliation: sarcastic verbal attacks, name-calling, and at its worst, verbal and physical violence.

Second, you may complain through *gossip*. Usually the gossip does not deliberately lie. Instead, he slanders by making negative reports, seeking to convince others that these reports are true. Complaining gossip divides brother against brother; indeed, that is the purpose—you want others on your side and against your offender. If you can convince some people that you are right, you can justify your resentment. "A perverse man stirs up dissension, and a gossip separates close friends" (Prov. 16:28).

A complainer sets himself up as judge, a position specifically forbidden us by Christ.

> Anyone who *speaks against his brother* or judges him, speaks against the law and judges it. . . . There is only one Lawgiver and Judge, the One who is able to save and destroy. But you—who are you to judge your neighbor? (James 4:11-12).

As a complaining gossip, you join the work of the devil, who accuses the brethren in order to divide them from God and each other (Rev. 12:10; cf. Job 1:8-12; 2:3-6). It

13

helps no one, but spreads discouragement like a disease; all the parties involved and the whole body of Christ grieve while the evil one rejoices. The Spirit says:

> Whoever spreads slander is a fool. . . . He who covers an offense promotes love, but whoever repeats the matter separates close friends (Prov. 10:18; 17:9).

> Love each other deeply, because love covers a multitude of sins (I Pet. 4:8).

Third, you may complain by assuming the role of *self-appointed "martyr."* You cover your complaint and gossip with a mantle of "injured innocence" as you appeal for understanding and sympathy. You talk as though you have to endure an unfair situation because you are "too weak or hurt to do anything else." You withdraw and begin quietly to obstruct the lives of those around you against whom your submerged anger is directed. What a grand strategy to win sympathy as a "victim" and yet marshal an attack, veiled in a cloak of "innocence"! If you are actually disabled, you might use that to reinforce your status as "victim." It is easy to convince yourself that you are helpless when actually you are rejecting godly help. Tragically, you forfeit great blessing for yourself and others by your unholy attempt to win pity. You sacrifice the joyous for the petty and infect those around you with frustration and discouragement.

Fourth, you may disguise *retaliation as "constructive criticism."* There is a difference between valid critique and sinful, harmful criticism. Your motive and manner are all-important. Appropriate, helpful criticism encourages as well as corrects. It is as clear and accurate as possible. Above all it is motivated by genuine love for and loyalty to the other person (see, for examples, II Tim. 2:24-26; 4:1-2; Philem.). However, criticism often becomes retaliation, as we simply vent our disappointment and resentment. We may try to feel better about ourselves by letting the other person know how bad we feel about him. Or we may "put down" a person to win an argument or conflict. Such criticism is sinful. Though a critic may use facts, if his motive or manner is sinful, so is his criticism, and it will usually create more confusion and harm. How much happier and more effective would we be in our homes, churches, and work places if our criticism were done with genuine grace.

For some people these more restrained forms of retaliation have become an ingrained habit. They instinctively strike back in any hurtful or threatening situation. The hypocrisy of such behavior should be clear, despite its commonness. Is it not one reason why we often forfeit God's blessing in our families and churches? A spirit of retaliation corrodes hope and engenders cynicism both for the parties involved in conflict and for those around who are touched by it. Children and new Christians are especially vulnerable to its harm.

Sometimes retaliating against current offenders has its root in underlying fear and anger that developed from earlier, unresolved conflicts. Although unconnected to a past experience, the current incident taps that reservoir of fear and anger. If you have symptoms of this within yourself, you must ask forgiveness for the behavior and seek insight into its causes. Common symptoms are these: frequent feelings of anger and depression without knowing why, fits of rage, violent reactions over trivial matters, and easily aroused resentment that lasts a long time. You need to forgive whoever caused the injury that lies behind this pain and anger. If that person is available, go to him and seek to work through the problem to forgiveness and reconciliation. However, if that person is dead or otherwise unavailable, you can still prayerfully resolve the matter before the Lord, genuinely forgiving the one who hurt you. You may need to work this out with a fellow disciple or Christian counselor. However hurt you are from the past, in Christ you need not be enslaved by it. You are responsible to deal with it; and you cannot use it to excuse behavior that hurts people now.

When you retaliate, you effectively reject any significant responsibility either for contributing to the original problem or for resolving it. You shift the fault, along with the burden for any resolution, onto the other person. Should that person seek forgiveness and reconciliation, he is often rebuffed. Not surprisingly, hopelessness overshadows our relationships when retaliation rules.

Jesus displayed this refusal to retaliate in His own crucifixion. Isaiah prophesied of Him, "As a sheep before her shearers is silent, so he did not open his mouth (53:7). The Holy Spirit relates this directly to us:

> If you suffer for doing good and you endure it, this is commendable before God. *To this you were called, because Christ suffered for you, leaving you an example, that you should follow in his steps.* "He committed no sin, and no deceit was found in his mouth." *When they hurled their insults at him, he did not retaliate; when he suffered, he made no threats.* Instead he trusted himself to [God] who judges justly. . . . Do not repay evil with evil or insult with insult, but with blessing, because to this you were called *so that you may inherit a blessing* (I Pet. 2:20b-23; 3:9, emphasis added).

Jesus' example brings us to the heart of the issue. It is more than a religious ideal to admire and then dismiss as impractical in "the real world." Jesus worked it out in the blood and pain of the real world, and so must we in following Him. Peter addresses the common situations where we often experience conflict and the temptation to strike back: relations with government officials, on-the-job strife, tensions in marriages and families and in the church family. Even more significant for us, Jesus' example is part of the gospel, God's creative word of promise. As by faith we submit to the lordship of Christ, the creative power of God works into our hearts what His Word requires us to work out in living. He makes obedience possible (see Phil. 2:1-16). Instead of retaliating, Jesus accepted the pain of His crucifixion and the anguish of bearing our sins. Can we not trust God's power in us and His care for us in order to obey Him? Can we not defer to His working out justice with righteousness and grace?

As it did for Jesus, our forgiving others means bearing increased pain for the sake of those we forgive instead of making them bear the pain of our anger and retaliation. Precisely at this point the complaint "It's not fair" collapses. God's will for us and those who fail us is not "fairness"; it is grace and mercy and faithfulness. Although our suffering does not win divine atonement (Jesus' sacrifice is unique), it does give us the right and motive to intercede for those who injure us—"Father, forgive them." In this way we participate in His granting forgiveness: "If you forgive anyone his sins, they are forgiven; if you do not forgive them, they are not forgiven" (John 20:23; cf. Matt. 18:18). There is mystery here, but the Word clearly connects *our* forgiving others and our ministering *God's* forgiveness. What an awesome responsibility and privilege! Doing this gives us a unique opportunity to communicate our Lord's grace: "Love each other as I have loved you. Greater love has no one than this, that he lay down his life for his friends" (John 15:12-13).

Bearing our brother's failure without resentment also creates the opportunity for our choicest fellowship with Jesus. We begin to enjoy "the fellowship of sharing in his sufferings, becoming like him in his death, and so, some-how, to attain to the resurrection from the dead" (Phil. 3:10-11). In His fellowship we find healing for our pain, and power and hope for a resolution in the present as well as in the future. Jesus comforts us:

> Come to me, all you who are weary and burdened, and I will give you rest. Take my yoke upon you and learn from me, for I am gentle and humble in heart, and you will find rest for your souls. For my yoke is easy and my burden is light (Matt. 11:28-30).

Bearing the pain of forgiveness is the way of faith—and of the cross—but it is also the way of Christ's richest bless-ing for the offended and the offender. Will we not trust Him? Is not that fellowship with Christ so precious that it makes resentment and retaliation an unthinkable alterna-tive?

IV.   FORGIVE SEVENTY-SEVEN TIMES?

Once the offender has received forgiveness, never bring up the offense again. Do not allow it to intrude on your continuing relationship with your now forgiven friend. Do not keep dwelling on it in your mind, or discuss it with others. True forgiveness is a *covenant act*, a promise by which we relinquish all claims against the offender that resulted from his sin. The righteous forgiver "keeps his oath even when it hurts" (Ps. 15:4). Thank God He treats us that way!

He does not treat us as our sins deserve or repay us according to our iniquities. For as high as the heavens are above the earth, so great is his love toward those who fear him; as far as the east is from the west, so far has he removed our transgressions from us (Ps. 103:10-12).

If you, O Lord, kept a record of sins, O Lord, who could stand? (Ps. 130:3).

I will forgive their wickedness and will remember their sins no more (Jer. 31:34; see also Heb. 10:15-17).

Frequently it is said, "I can forgive, but I can never forget." Actually this cliché misses the point; the issue is not forgetting but forgiving. The notion of "forgive and forget" implies abandoning rather than healing the relationship. One may actually intend *not* to forget, as a defense. Scripture calls us to forgive *and reconcile,* which renders defense unnecessary. Working through the issue to reconciliation will help bring healing from pain, but the actual emotional memory of a serious offense may take some time to forget. Because forgetting is sometimes very hard, making the conscious faith commitment to forgive and reconcile and never raise the issue again is strategically important. Our commitment must override memory and feelings; this begins both faithfulness and healing. However, beyond these things—and even if the offender refuses to be reconciled—we must seek our spiritual healing in deeper fellowship with Christ.

Often with our children or with others over whom we have authority, we err at this point. We frequently remind them of their sins and errors, hoping to maintain control and keep them from doing something else displeasing. This in effect is a form of retaliation; we use their past failures against them. Such tactics do not work; instead they incite further resistance in those under us and multiply our frustration. Moreover, when constantly reminded of their failures, people, especially children and others who feel weak, become disheartened, give up, and withdraw. The problems are only perpetuated, and we sacrifice fellowship, unity, and productivity. And yet, we in authority often continue to blame those under us, never seeing our own basic failure. Do we not sometimes fear that if we really forgive people and treat them graciously, they will take advantage of us? In that fear we sin against those for whom God has made us responsible, and against God Himself. We demonstrate that we lack faith in God's grace and power, and depend, instead, on rigid rules and demands to control others. And when our expectations are not met, we compound our problems with mutual resentment and retaliation. The Word urges husbands and parents, employers, and elders to avoid this tendency (see Eph. 5:25-33; 6:4, 9; Col. 3:19, 21; 4:1; I Pet. 5:2-3).

But what if the offender does repeat the sin?

> Then Peter came to Jesus and asked, "Lord, how many times shall I forgive my brother when he sins against me? Up to seven times?" (Matt. 18:21).

If a sin is repeated, may we not bring up that previous offense? No! We must not hold a *forgiven* sin against someone, nor may we retract previous forgiveness because of the present sin; in this sense the old forgiven incident remains closed.

We can share Peter's frustration! What then are we to do? Jesus puts it clearly, "I tell you not seven times but seventy-seven times," that is, without limitation (Matt. 18:22). He then reinforces the point with the parable about a king who condemns his indebted servant because the servant, although he had been treated kindly by the king, was harsh and unforgiving to his fellow-servant. Jesus concludes the parable with this warning: "This is how my heavenly Father will treat each of you unless you forgive your brother from your heart" (Matt. 18:35).

How then can we deal with the problem of repeated offenses despite previous forgiveness? We begin by realistically understanding that sins are never isolated acts; they flow out of the sinfulness of the heart. Many sins—for example, outbursts of anger, crude or abusive language, thoughtlessness and rudeness, and worry—involve deeply ingrained habit patterns of thought, emotional response, and behavior. Though they are not for that reason excusable, they do call for a persevering and patient ministry. To keep a just perspective, we all must remember that we too struggle in the Spirit with sinfulness within, even though we may not be guilty of the particular failure that offends us. (For more on spiritual growth, consider Gal. 5:22–6:2 and II Pet. 1:3-11.)

Until this ingrained aspect of a sin is dealt with, repetition is likely. Many times, in the process of reconciliation, we focus too narrowly on resolving a specific incident. But when the offense is serious and reflects a sinful pattern, *we must also address heart attitudes and outline steps to take to break the sinful habit.* If a counselor is involved, he must ensure that his counselee faces these underlying issues along with the specific offense. Sincere confession of a specific incident does not solve the problem; the offender must also build new habits as he comes to grips with the underlying factors. *However, Jesus makes it clear that we cannot make our forgiveness conditional on some assurance that the offense will never happen again.* We should work and pray to reduce the likelihood of recurrence, but we must forgive the specific act even though we lack a warranty against recurrence.

21

V. RETURN BLESSING FOR HURT

Commit yourself to doing good for the offender. The Lord charges us,

> Love your enemies, do good to those who hate you, bless those who curse you, pray for those who mistreat you. . . . that you may be sons of your Father in heaven" (Luke 6:27; Matt. 5:45; cf. v. 44).

Doing good for those who offend us is not conditioned on successful reconciliation. It applies even when the offender has refused restoration, when he continues to be hostile. Replace antagonism with prayer and blessing in your heart and behavior. This breaks the cycle of retaliation, and often, by the grace of God, it fosters reconciliation. Even if that does not occur, we must use every opportunity to show God's grace as His children. Replacing retaliation with blessing, the Scripture instructs us:

> Do not repay anyone evil for evil. Be careful to do what is right in the eyes of everybody. If it is possible, as far as it depends on you, live at peace with everyone. Do not take revenge, my friends, but leave room for God's wrath, for it is written, "It is mine to avenge; I will repay," says the Lord. *On the contrary: "If your enemy is hungry, feed him; if he is thirsty, give him something to drink. . . ."* Do not be overcome by evil, but overcome evil with good (Rom. 12:17-21, emphasis added).

(For more on this, see the excellent little book by Jay E. Adams, *How to Overcome Evil* [Phillipsburg, N.J.: Presbyterian and Reformed, 1977]).

VI.   A LOVING SPIRIT

Develop a loving spirit slow to respond to offenses. We must commit ourselves to grow in loving other people as we grow in our experience of God's love for us.

Dear friends, let us love one another, for love comes from God. Everyone who loves has been born of God and knows God. Whoever does not love does not know God, because God is love. This is how God showed his love among us: he sent his one and only Son into the world that we might live through him. This is love: not that we loved God, but that he loved us and sent his Son as an atoning sacrifice for our sins. Dear friends, since God so loved us, we also ought to love one another. No one has ever seen God; but if we love each other, God lives in us and his love is made complete in us (I John 4:7-12).

A loving spirit begins with God's love in our hearts. Developing this loving spirit is one practical aspect of working out the biblical teaching on the church. In the congregation of Jesus Christ our bonds to one another in Christ—not our negative instincts and narrow self-interest—must determine our attitudes, choices, and behavior. God Himself bonds us together in the church. We are not a "voluntary" social organization. God has made us a *covenant* community by His word of promise and His Holy Spirit. We are responsible to Him for our life both corporately as the church and separately within individual families and as individual members. Trusting the Holy Spirit, we must order our living on His principles:

If you have any encouragement from being united with Christ, if any comfort from his love, if any fellowship with the Spirit, if any tenderness and compassion, then make my joy complete by being like-minded, having the same love, being one in spirit and purpose. Do nothing out of selfish ambition or vain conceit, but in humility consider others better than yourselves. Each of you should look not only to your own interest, but also to the interests of others. Your attitude should be the same as that of Christ Jesus (Phil. 2:1-5).

Live a life worthy of the calling you have received. Be completely humble and gentle; be patient, bearing with one another in love. Make every effort to keep the unity of the Spirit through the bond of peace. . . . Submit to one another out of reverence for Christ (Eph. 4:1b-3; 5:21).

Love is patient, love is kind. It does not envy, it does not boast, it is not proud. It is not rude, it is not self-seeking, it is not easily angered, it keeps no record of wrongs. Love does not delight in evil but rejoices with the truth. It always protects, always trusts, always hopes, always perseveres (I Cor. 13:4-7).

We who are strong ought to bear with the failings of the weak and not to please ourselves. Each of us should please his neighbor for his good, to build him up. For even Christ did not please himself but, as it is written, "The insults of those who insult you have fallen on me" (Rom. 15:1-3).

Make sure that nobody pays back wrong for wrong, but always try to be kind to each other and to everyone else (I Thess. 5:15).

This bond, or covenant, is as much the law of God as

the Ten Commandments or the Sermon on the Mount. In fact, it is in this context that we understand these great specific statements of law; the church God created with His covenant is the first arena in which we live out His commandments. Failing there, we can never succeed in the larger world that is already hostile to God and His church (see John 15:18-21). Faith expressing itself through love fulfills the law (Gal. 5:6; Rom. 13:10). The promise to forgive works within this broad covenant relationship established by Christ. (See Eph. 2:11-22 for more on Christ's establishing the covenant people through His sacrifice.) Our forgiving follows the pattern established by God in His covenant of redemption.

Four further aspects of developing a forgiving spirit are these:

First, ignore incidental and trivial irritation; do not create a personal offense where none really exists or was intended. "A fool shows his annoyance at once, but a prudent man overlooks an insult" (Prov. 12:16). For example, someone may not speak to you during the fellowship time after morning worship. To take offense means that you impose on that oversight the worst possible interpretation and react accordingly. People who do this usually cling dogmatically to their negative judgments, never recognizing that they create or magnify offenses in their own imaginations. Instead, determine to see things people do or omit in the best possible way. "Love . . . believes all things, hopes all things" (I Cor. 13:7, NASB).

Second, work on clear and loving communication, in which not only do you transfer information but you also convey gentle, caring patience (see II Tim. 2:23-26). We are all fallible and limited in our perspectives; misunderstandings and differences are inevitable. When these occur, rather

25

than reacting negatively and defensively, *listen,* and work patiently through to understanding each other. We will not always agree with each other, but, when we do disagree, we can maintain loyal and caring fellowship. When you respond, strive first to *"benefit* those who listen." If you have difficulty coming to a working agreement with someone, then together share the matter with brethren who can help sort it out. For Christians, our most basic aim is to encourage, to use every opportunity for strengthening unity, fellowship, and holiness—because we are one in Jesus Christ.

Third, learn to be "content in any and every situation" (Phil. 4:12b). A complaining spirit has its heart in the world, and "friendship with the world is hatred toward God" (James 4:4). A person who is always grumbling and feels generally dissatisfied is readily defensive ("touchy"), easily offended, and easily discouraged. He has little practical faith in God's care. Envy and resentment lie close to the surface. The contented Christian finds his rest and security in the grace and care of the Lord and his purpose in serving God's kingdom. He is free to bear with and care for the brethren. We must abandon the "play-it-safe-for-me" attitude. We must confront in ourselves the self-centered tendency to be discontented whenever things go awry. We must replace discontent with generosity, caring, and hospitality. Make this a matter of regular prayer, spiritual discipline, and mutual encouragement. The Spirit says to the churches:

> Do everything without complaining or arguing, so that you may become blameless and pure, children of God without fault in a crooked and depraved generation, in which you shine like stars in the universe as you hold out the word of life (Phil. 2:14-16a).

Fourth, rejoice consistently in the wonderful grace of God—
and that not only when your situation prospers and everyone around is at peace with you, but also in times of trial and
stress. A rejoicing, thankful heart has little room for resentment, little of the energy required to retaliate. This, of
course, brings us back to faith—we must believe in God's
grace to us not only when things are pleasant but also when
they get tough. We must fix our hearts on His promise "that
in all things God works for the good of those who love him,
who have been called according to his purpose. . . . to be
conformed to the likeness of his Son" (Rom. 2:28, 29). The
Holy Spirit clearly shows us that rejoicing in faith and a
gracious spirit go together:

> Rejoice in the Lord always. I will say it again: Rejoice!
> Let your gentleness be evident to all. The Lord is near.
> Do not be anxious about anything, but in everything,
> by prayer and petition, with thanksgiving, present your
> requests to God. And the peace of God, which tran-
> scends all understanding, will guard your hearts and
> your minds in Christ Jesus (Phil. 4:4-7).

Impossible, you think? Remember Paul wrote those
words in a situation where we might expect him to be
frustrated, angry, and eager to retaliate. Paul was unjustly
in prison, "in chains for Christ." Even worse, some profess-
ing to be Christians were using his imprisonment to stir up
trouble for him, preaching out of envy, rivalry, and selfish
ambition. But Paul, focusing on God's grace, rejoiced, and
he calls us to do so as well (Phil. 1:12-18). Let the joy of
Christ fill your heart so that you will be slow to respond
negatively to people, slow to take offense, and eager to
forgive.

FORGIVE AS WE ARE FORGIVEN

Jesus calls us to this as disciples. Jesus Christ has given us His Spirit to bring about in us what pleases Him. What He has begun in us He will perfect until the day of Christ. We can do all things through the strength He gives. Only rebellion born of unbelief, cynicism, and self-pity will refuse His gracious command.

What about our children? The natural tendency to retaliate rather than forgive shows itself early in life. However, children have a natural "lab," the Christian family, in which to learn forgiveness. Obviously this learning depends heavily on Christian parents' practicing forgiveness both within and outside the home. Parents have many opportunities to encourage their children to trust their heavenly Father and follow what He says in His Word. This begins as parents model a godly relationship with each other before their children and extend that to the children themselves. Child discipline must come out of love with gentleness, clarity, and firmness, always accompanied by forgiveness, a forgiveness not to be withdrawn at their next failure. (How often even we Christian parents must ask both God and our children for forgiveness at this point!) (For more on the loving discipline of children, see *Withhold Not Correction* by Pastor Bruce Ray [Phillipsburg, N.J.: Presbyterian and Reformed, 1978].)

When children offend each other, those offenses may seem devastating to them, even though to us they appear trivial. Children often need our help to gain control of their feelings and find a kind, helpful response. If Johnny is caught stealing his sister's allowance, he is chastised and made to return the money, but this "justice" will not of itself restore their loving, trusting relationship. He needs to ask

28

her to forgive him, and she, to respond positively. They often need for Dad or Mom gently to encourage them to do this. Children too can learn that our goal is not merely justice—or "getting even"—but also caring and reconciliation.

What of Martha and Jim, with whose conflict we began our discussion? The story presents only one side, but they both obviously need respect for God's will and trust in His grace. Then they can work toward deep forgiveness and a reconciliation that deals with self-centered and harmful behavior and with bitterness and resentment. They are not unique; sadly Christians sometimes *do* "do things like that." However, they can find hope in the grace and Word of God.

Forgiveness is neither "natural" nor easy for us. Even though the principles are clear, our residual sinfulness in a fallen world complicates our practice of them. In pride and stubbornness we simply may not *want* to forgive. We often fail to trust God's care enough to obey as we protest, "I can't do it!" We need each other in the body to help us at this point, to give us encouragement and sometimes even rebuke.

> Brothers, if someone is caught in a sin, you who are spiritual should restore him gently. But watch yourself, or you also may be tempted. Carry each other's burdens, and this way you will fulfill the law of Christ (Gal. 6:1-2).

When the entrapping sin is a refusal to forgive, we must be sensitive to the pain and fear that often lie beneath it. We must give support and comfort, encouraging our fellow-disciple to trust his Lord's grace and power: "I can do everything through Christ who gives me strength" (Phil. 3:13). But we must also keep before him the Lord's command. Easy or not, Christ both commands and makes possible forgiving those who offend us, who sin against us, whose faults and failures get under our skin. The Holy Spirit writes this command into our hearts as He confirms to us God's forgiveness; it is for us now to trust and obey.

As God's chosen people, holy and dearly loved, clothe yourselves with compassion, kindness, humility, gentleness and patience. Bear with each other and forgive whatever grievances you may have against one another. Forgive as the Lord forgave you (Col. 3:12-14).